TRAVELING WITH THE FATES

Vignettes from a trip to Greece

Peter Stathopoulos

Cover design by Lauren Stathopoulos
Cover photo atop Palamidi fortress, Nafplion, Greece,
by John Stathopoulos

Portions of Chapter One originally appeared in the
St. Paul Pioneer Press.
Chapter Five, in modified form, originally appeared in the
New York Times.

ISBN: 9798673011478
Design by Pen2publishing

I dedicate this book to John, Nikos and Maria Stathopoulos, my travel companions through Greece and life.

And to Terri, who lit my heart that night on Hydra and to this day.

Table of Contents

Some say an army on horseback,

some say an army on foot,
and some say a fleet of ships is the most beautiful thing on
this dark earth.

But I say it is whatever you love.

Sappho of Lesbos, approximately 580 BC

Prologue

When I was 19 and all it took to travel was a hitch-hiker's thumb, a willingness to sleep anywhere, plus harmonica skills to pull in money for food and train rides, I backpacked Europe with the simple goal of taking in raw images for my brain to polish over the years into something "meaningful" – whatever that might mean.

When I was middle-aged and had a regular job, travel meant exploring different sites and foods and languages with my family, tasting the beautiful diversity of foreign cities and building shared memories.

I pictured variations of the same in my older years, enjoying the glow of twilight with my wife, reminiscing on raising our kids and taking joy in tales of their travels through adulthood, both their tangible odysseys and those that take place in their hearts and minds.

Divorce erased the promise of twilight reminiscences with their mother, but it didn't change the magic of traveling with my kids. Twenty-three-year-old John had returned to Minnesota after five years exploring the mountains and himself in Montana, while my 18-year-old twins, Nikos and Maria, were heading off to college in New York and Chicago.

I booked a trip I had long dreamt of taking with them but never quite gotten around to doing, waiting for the perfect time. We would visit Greece to explore its ancient cities and seaside villages, casually seek traces of our ancestors and, most important, enjoy leisurely days just hanging out before their lives took off with college and careers.

I realized this sort of time-out-of-time together would soon be limited by the logistics of their lives blossoming in multiple directions. Five days before we left for Greece, my diagnosis with ALS revealed just how limited it was.

CHAPTER 1

Fountain of Life

While it's hard to tell an Angel from a Muse, one of the two phoned me at an Athens apartment on a hot July morning. Steam rising from the swimming pool below our balcony misted my view and put me in a frame of mind for magic.

"Mr. Stathopoulos, I have news about the monastery you want to visit with your children," Erato said.

"Good news, I trust."

"Well, it closed 20 years ago."

"Impossible," I shook off the mist. "We were there in 1997, my ex-wife and I."

"Okay, 19 years and change," she humored me. "Now here's your good news: The monastery is finally open again."

"How about the miracle fountain?"

"Yes, it reopened three weeks ago."

"Beautiful, let's go today!"

Erato paused, "Unfortunately, it's impossible for you to get there."

"I'm still healthy enough to hike," I assured her and myself.

"The entire mountain is now closed."

"You're kidding, right?"

"It's too hot, too windy. We've had no rain this summer. The government is afraid of forest fires so close to the city. Nobody is allowed up there except the rangers."

"Is there another way in?" I asked. There was nothing I wanted more on this trip.

"You're in Athens another week. Sometimes it opens for a few hours and closes all of a sudden. I'll call to check every morning, but no promises," the angel promised.

I felt a sun ray of hope – not for a cure but for one more round of magic with my kids.

Nineteen years ago my then-wife and I hiked up Mount Hymettus past tinfoil-lined grottos, stray cats and giant beehives to a Byzantine monastery surrounded by tall thin cypress trees. Behind the monastery stood a ram's head fountain that women had drank from for fertility long before monasteries existed.

Nine months later we had twins.

I had always wanted to show this place to our kids. Now with time running out, the want felt like a need.

Erato called again two days later, "Mount Hymettus is open this morning, but it will shut down again this afternoon. Can you and the children be ready in an hour?"

"We're ready now."

"Great, your driver is on his way."

The drive was familiar and not. Two decades ago we walked an hour across Athens from the Acropolis to get to the mountain at the edge of the city. This time, my kids and I were chauffeured in from Kifisia, an Athens suburb.

Still I found wide clean boulevards lined by messy storefronts and concrete-slab apartment buildings that looked like they had been thrown up as speedily as possible – which was exactly what happened when Athens needed to make room for a million ethnic Greeks who got kicked out of Turkey a century ago.

Plane trees and cypress trees lining the boulevard completed the sense of being in a place that was Western and Middle Eastern at once.

I looked but didn't see the amusement park in a vacant lot with a small old-fashioned Ferris wheel like you used to see in American Midwestern county fairs. It had probably been temporary in the first place, which I suppose everything is – making monuments like the Acropolis and fountains women have visited for thousands of years even more amazing.

Our driver Haralambos – "call me Harry" – wound up the road through the pine forest toward the monastery. I almost told him, "Stop, please. We want to walk up from the bottom." But I didn't, knowing I should save my energy.

He dropped us off with bottles of drinking water 300 feet downhill from the monastery and asked, "Are you okay walking from here?" My eyes must have flashed because he quickly explained, "Most people want me to drive them as close as I can."

"Thanks, I want to take it in one breath at a time."

We walked crunching dead pine needles under a bright blue sky up to the entrance where a man in a lightweight cardigan taking offerings looked pleasantly surprised to see visitors.

I immediately recalled everything except for one: "Where is the fountain?"

John, solid as a mountain man in sunglasses, a sea-blue T-shirt and blue jeans, shook his head as if to say, "Hey, it's not for me."

The monastery guy glanced curiously at vibrant, olive-skinned Maria with her hair pulled up. A crossover purse dangled over her black-and-white striped top and dark green shorts. Then he shifted his gaze to her energetic hazel-eyed twin Nikos in curly black hair, a blue tie-dyed shirt and khaki shorts. None of them appeared to need extra fertility, so he looked back at me.

"They were kind of born there," I explained.

"It's out around the back," his voice had the soft glow of one who spends his days contemplating joy. "I can show you now or we can walk back there together when you leave."

The Kaisariani Monastery grounds appeared as they did in my memory. Cats napped and flowers burst from cracks in the stone pathways that meandered on a human scale. The idea was to inspire contemplation rather than to impress.

Cats made their way to Nikos in the courtyard as they do everywhere. He's had a way with animals since being bit in the eye by a cocker spaniel as a toddler – they see their gentlest selves in him. Now at the monastery he sat on a stone-slab bench and held cat court, petting and welcoming all, while Maria and John roamed.

The Byzantine frescoes on the walls and ceiling of the dim round chapel where I sat were more vivid than I remembered, thanks to years of restoration – 20 years, as Erato had told me – with tools the size of toothbrushes and needles. Colors were gold like in children's glow pens, faces too symmetrical. Simplicity is moving when it strikes without warning, as is sincerity.

I sat in the dark stone chapel remembering the optimism from early in my marriage: We would treasure travel over trinkets, time over money; we'd have love so full it would leave no room for boredom. A winter picture came to me: Walking across Walgreens parking lot in a snowstorm to get milk with three-month-old John in my arms, an ancient woman in a walker and snug white hat beaming at us. She knew the magic.

More snapshots flooded in, along with questions light and dark for which there was no single answer.

And the birth of our miraculous twins, of course, whether you believe in Miracles or miracles...

Now in the silent chapel I caught myself mumbling, a little embarrassed although only I could hear: "One more miracle would be kind of nice."

After a moment or eternity, we left the monastery and wandered around back to the fertility fountain. My twins humored me by posing for a photo, with Maria treating me to an excellent eye roll when I solemnly warned her not to drink.

We continued up Mount Hymettus where the pine forest grew thinner, my grown kids running ahead and then pausing for me. Nikos sprinted and leapt up to the next plateau like a tall, lean goat. His whimsical spirit is much like mine had been until the years rusted its edges. People who knew me at his age tell the poor kid that he not only looks like I did, but also moves and talks and sees the world like me.

Maria wandered into a cave that held a grotto lined with tinfoil and decorated with paper cutouts of Jesus and Mary. John stood with his thumbs in his blue jean pockets checking out the view down the mountain to the sea in one direction, the city of Athens in another and undulating hills all around.

The ancient Greeks came to Mount Hymettus for its honey and also to seek omens: Clouds forming in the shape of a horse meant war was coming; a ship sailing into the harbor sideways meant more than just sea winds were changing fast; a thunderbolt out of the clear blue sky promised beauty or disaster – not that the two are mutually exclusive.

A hawk screeched overhead from our right, the direction of good in Ancient Greece and in many cultures today, then circled to our left.

My eyes roved to four lush cypress trees, standing the way families do in too-stiff portraits, three kid trees plus a mature dad tree on the end. I pulled out my i-phone and photographed the healthy family of trees, an omen I might survive this disease that nobody in history had beaten.

With my phone back in my pocket, I took a deep breath and gazed through the trees to the valley below us and the mountaintops across the way. Then I stared directly at the row of deep-green cypresses to lock the picture in my head as well as my camera.

Something I hadn't noticed looking at my phone:

A dead brown tree stood right in the middle.

What kind of idiot believes in omens anyway?

Watching John and Maria step around rocks and climb over fallen tree trunks to join Nikos higher up the pine forest mountain, I just plain felt good. Since he was born, Nikos has had a gift for living in the moment; my mind's eye saw the green leaves of a rare deciduous tree there on the mountain sparkle under his gaze.

Thirsty and happy and in no hurry, we made our way down to the spot on the mountain where Harry had dropped us off. He put his cigarette out on a boulder and gave us fresh iced bottles of water from a cooler in the car.

"What did you think of the monastery?"

"Beautiful in every way," I said.

"Did you visit the fountain?"

"We did."

"Just about every town in Greece has a monastery where they claim to cure barren women," he shook his head.

"Every town probably has a place that claims to make ice cream, too," I said.

"Yes, but I can see the ice cream," Harry argued.

"And I can see these kids," I nodded to Nikos and Maria while our car wound down Mount Hymettus.

CHAPTER 2

Counting Sheep

It's one thing to tell myself it's not worth obsessing over whether I'll live or die because I will certainly die. We all will. It's another to find this comforting enough to put me to sleep a week after my terminal diagnosis: ALS, Lou Gehrig's disease, life expectancy two years, paralysis in all limbs sooner. The claustrophobia of being trapped inside my own body.

With the full moon creeping in through the window as palpably as the hot July breeze, I pace near the screen door in our apartment thinking about a story by Jorge Luis Borges: the narrator visualizes every possible way that he might die, confident that if he imagines it ahead of time, it can't possibly happen that way.

Then terror strikes: If he imagines a specific death, that is exactly how he'll die.

So many ways to go with ALS: The standard lung failure if you make it that far, but you might be spared via an earlier final bell: choking on a piece of pizza; aspirating a sip of juice; a heart attack after a summer's nap while a fresh breeze slides through the window. There's also stroke, suicide, pneumonia... too many ways to count as the moon soars.

Aging speeds up with ALS like in a time elapse film clip. Your arms quit, your neck droops, you walk hunched over, your legs go, you can't eat or speak, you gasp for air and die – not necessarily in that order, except for the last one.

For better or for worse, your mind stays solid unless you get dementia or let yourself go nuts.

What's the first thing you see after your breath stops? Jesus, Buddha? My grandpa Ray, who used to lurk behind the bedroom door and pretend to be a ghost?

And what comes next?

If you ask the blind poet Homer from 3000 years ago, the Greek warrior Achilles gave King Odysseus the scoop when the king visited him in Hades: "I would rather be the most wretched slave on earth than to be a king in the land of the dead."

I grew up Lutheran so my afterlife is happier than that. I'm counting on harp lessons with a lovely girl, a bottomless Communion wine glass, and a knowing smile when my grandkids hear thunder and say, "Sounds like the angels are bowling again."

My old college roommate Ken said it better: "I have a feeling that when we get to the other side we're going to look around and say, *Was it really this simple all along?*"

Down on the street, John and Nikos dash between cars and motorbikes to cross the busy road for late-night souvlaki and French fries stuffed in warm pita bread at Bobby's all-night café. Maria leans on the railing of our apartment's large balcony gazing out at the city lights and silhouettes of mountains. Our laundry sways on the balcony clothesline.

I think I smell the meat grilling from Bobby's across the street, but that's not it. John and Nikos are back already, opening the apartment door carrying heaping gyro sandwiches wrapped in aluminum foil, which we take outside to eat on the balcony.

I wonder if I'll get to know these astonishing people in the next place. Will we wear the same or different faces?

Back in bed, a breeze rustles the curtains. The clock says 3 a.m., I'm wide awake.

I think I'll take up counting sheep. They're pretty and it's the Greek way.

CHAPTER 3

On the Road to Delphi

Omens are bogus, of course, and trying to prevent your death by imagining it is even stupider. But an Oracle, now that's somewhere you can place your faith – just ask 3400 years of kings and fools and those who wore both crowns.

I had wanted to visit the Oracle at Delphi back when I was my twins' age. But the location didn't fit my formula of thumbing it by day and taking trains by night so the train could double as a hotel. Delphi wasn't on a good hitchhiking route and no trains went there, so I didn't go either.

Now as an old man before my time, I heard my angel's voice again: "Mr. Stathopoulos, good morning."

"Erato!"

"We're all set for your visit to Delphi. I'm sure it will have lots to tell you. Harry will pick you and the children up in an hour. It's a stunning drive across the countryside and up to Mount Parnassus. Your guide will be Sophie. She's our best. She grew up right in the village of Delphi."

Tourists either loved the Oracle at Delphi or found it to be a boring barren ruin in the middle of nowhere. I knew already I was going to love it. In addition to finding ruins more interesting than standing buildings any day, the comedy of how great kings made their decisions, and still do, was too amusing to pass up.

Warlords crossed deserts, seas and jagged mountains from as far away as Persia so they could beg teenage girls stoned on underground gases to tell them the future.

The girls mumbled to a priest who culled their chorus down to sayings so vague that in hindsight they were always true – think of them as the original consulting group.

In 547 BC King Croesus of Lydia – roughly modern day Turkey – got sick of the Persian Empire lurking at his eastern border.

Even though the Persian army was much bigger, Croesus figured he could take them down. Persian soldiers wore pants, for one thing, not skirts like the manly Lydians.

Before starting a war against the world's strongest army, though, he wanted to be sure. So he traveled to Delphi to ask the teenage girls and their priest.

"Yes, invade Persia and you will destroy a great empire."

Confident the gods were on his side, Croesus' army attacked Persia. Unfortunately for Croesus, within days the Persian army captured him, bound him hand and foot with vines, taunted him then burned him on a pile of weeds, overran his country and turned the manly Lydians into slaves.

When Croesus' emissary went back to confront the priest for his false prophecy, the priest just shrugged, "I didn't say which empire."

We had an hour before our driver Harry would arrive to take us to Delphi. So the kids and I paused for the delightful morning confusion at the bakery 50 feet down the street from our apartment.

John pointed at the chocolate croissants and honey-layered pastries in the glass case – that was easy enough.

The adventure of ordering coffee came next. We turned to Nikos and Maria, who spoke the language best thanks to their Greek dance troupe.

Would we like our coffee hot, cold, black, with milk, sugar, straight? The twins knew the words in Greek, but in the delightful pandemonium misplaced them. I'm sure the women behind the counter knew the words in English, too, but we were all laughing too hard over the confusion, and our pronunciation could have come from different planets.

Each day, and each different barista who made the coffee, opened a new Babel: frappe, simple black, au lait, and every single cup was delicious because it was here, and they were exuberantly Greek, and we had all the hallmarks of the ugly American – pointing, talking loud, not knowing a word of their language when we needed it most – except we all brought the same spirit to the counter.

John tried to tip the woman at the register. She slid it back across the counter at him, lowering her eyes because she found him ruggedly cute in his short black hair, trimmed beard and solid biceps under a short-sleeve button-down shirt. John never saw the look in her eyes; he shyly looked away, too.

It wasn't a stingy tip. The second day, she accepted the tip. The third, she or her comrade shoved it back again, every time with a coy smile saying the puzzle of trying to figure us out was worth far more than bits of change – all this in a country whose economy was famously in shambles.

Energized with coffee and pastries, we got into Harry's car and headed across the city's concrete outskirts through industrial suburbs. Soon we would cross the countryside before ascending into the mountains and eventually Mount Parnassus, the gods' vacation home when they weren't scuffling on Mount Olympus.

During our drives we talked about a lot of things. On this one Harry told us the difference between the police in Greece and America: Unlike in America, Harry explained, Greek policemen can't just shoot somebody for no reason. Nikos agreed it's best to have a reason if you're going to shoot someone, and we sped along past concrete walls with graffiti and with wildflowers spilling through the cracks.

Towns along the highway grew more industrial before opening into long deep valleys and mountains clothed in pine and olive trees.

I looked forward to seeing what the Oracle at Delphi would tell me after my Omen of Dead Tree. It was possible I misread the dry brown cypress tree behind the monastery as drastically as Lydia's King Croesus had misinterpreted the message 2600 years ago.

The dead tree wasn't necessarily me. It could have been so many things. My marriage had died two years earlier after a decade on its deathbed, and my dog had passed three years ago.

Who knows how long the brown tree had been standing there? It didn't even look like me.

With thousands of years hindsight, I knew the Oracle at Delphi's message would be delivered so ambiguously that I could interpret it however I wanted.

Just 30 minutes outside of Athens, I realized I wasn't going to have to wait for Delphi.

The tollway exit sign pointed to a two-lane highway: Marathon 47 km.

I've never visited Marathon and never will, although I have read the guidebooks that describe it as "a modern industrial city with little to offer the traveler despite its obvious historical significance."

Marathon's significance for tourists is the 490 BC battle between the Persians and Athenians, brought to us by the ancient historian Herodotus, known as "The Father of History and Lies" and later adorned by Plutarch and other writers.

Herodotus' war stories are consistent with battlefield ruins and his contemporaries, while his tales of Egyptian ants big enough to devour a camel in one bite are suspect. In Herodotus' defense, he made it clear he didn't see the giant ants with his own eyes.

At the battle of Marathon, the Persian army slaughtered their way to within 26.2 miles of Athens and had the Greeks outnumbered by 100,000 Persians to 10,000 remaining Greeks.

The Greeks would have had 20,000 soldiers except the Spartans (the most notorious Greek warriors) refused to come help because they had an inviolable religious festival going on or, if you ask the Athenians, because the fear of fighting 100,000 Persians made them fill their skirts.

The Persian army charged across the Marathon valley, surprising even their puffed-up selves how easy it was after the resistance the Greeks had put up in earlier battles. Unfortunately for the Persians, the best Athenian warriors stood hidden in the surrounding mountains.

Once the Persians reached the point of no return, the Greeks streamed down the mountains from both sides, hacking thousands and sending the rest hiking up their pants and running back to their ships.

Pheidippides, a Greek soldier who fought in the battle, sprinted 26.2 miles in full metal armor back to Athens to announce the victory. As soon as he announced it, he fell dead of exhaustion.

What does all this mean?

It depends who you ask.

It also depends where you're at in life.

For me, a 19-year-old romantic who was thousands of years removed from the blood-soaked daggers and the life-or-death fight for Western civilization, it was a love story totally misinterpreted by Herodotus and every historian since then.

In a tale I wrote back when I was embarrassed about being a sap so threw it away, Pheidippides didn't die of exhaustion. Approaching Athens' city gates, he saw his lover in the arms of another man.

He died of heartbreak.

The poor hero had no way of knowing Daphne leapt into the first arms she could find because she was overcome with joy seeing him return from war alive.

Now at age 55 and with the clock ticking faster, looking back on my life for some kind of meaning, a different view of Marathon danced through my mind.

Pheidippides had just fought and won an against-all-odds battle that, if lost, would have wiped out Athens. He was a warrior.

If someone told him that 2500 years later almost nobody would know or care that he was part of a longshot victory that paved the way for Socrates, the Acropolis, America, Europe... that instead his legacy would be a 26-mile run and a face plant...

He would have laughed in their face if he were alive to do so.

We can't know what our legacy will be.

But here's to long-shot victories. More than ever, I'm all for those.

CHAPTER 4

Can You Hear Me, Major Tom?

The screen door to my bedroom balcony is wide open. Cicadas chirp and night birds sing between the rumble of motorcycles outside our Athens apartment.

My head sweats gloriously on the pillow as I lay wondering what my kids will remember when I'm gone:

I hope it's tossing a football in the front yard with John, playing chess at the kitchen table while thunder roars outside; kicking soccer balls across a green wet field with Nikos, playing cars and trucks on the floor; sitting on the couch with Maria finding faces in swift-moving clouds at dawn, walking home together from the tennis courts breathless at dusk, doing nothing at all... more than the late-evening emails and phone calls that were the price of being the single income in a single-income family.

As a breeze through the balcony doorway softens the night, fasciculations flow up and down my body like the pulsing of the sea baptizing Greece.

What is a fasciculation? It's a fancy word for what happens when your nerves and muscles try frantically to connect, while the nerves await signals from your dying motor neurons.

Think of your muscles as David Bowie's Major Tom, losing contact with the brain over a period of 1+ years and then dying.

People describe fasciculations as a sensation of ants crawling in your veins, but it doesn't feel that way to me lying in bed, nor when I get up to go stand on the balcony and breathe in the night. To me it's tiny pieces of bubble wrap popping randomly through my limbs.

The only limb where I don't feel it is my right arm, because once the nerves die the popping stops. For the past few days, I've felt it rolling through my left arm and both of my legs, but tonight it's different.

Tonight my chest pops, too. This is bothersome because 80% of people with ALS die of respiratory complications.

A friend told me ALS hustles around your body limb-to-limb as if rounding a baseball diamond before attacking the muscles that support the lungs. Based on my chest tonight, I suspect he overplayed the base-running analogy.

The beauty and the beast of this disease is that nobody has ever been cured, so there's little value in spastically running around deciding what to do. Just treasure every moment... there's a reason for the cliché.

I get up and pace the balcony with a glass of ice water on this hot dry night, listening to thousands of cicadas and thinking how I have forever to live compared to them.

I'm thinking, too, how joyful it is to hear John and Nikos through the open kitchen window, sharing a nightcap.

And how tomorrow I'll walk Athens with my kids, something I've dreamt of doing for so many years.

CHAPTER 5

Let Me Walk like Socrates

&

"Dad, I love this place!" dark-eyed Maria made my day with those five words. "It's different from anyplace I've ever been."

I knew exactly what she meant: Athens is a big contradictory city that feels neither 1st World nor 3rd World, nor even a combination of the two, but something altogether different.

The city piles up 3,000-year old marble masterpieces, Byzantine melodrama, modern concrete slabs that are all a poor city can afford, joy and pain, shrimp so fresh it melts in your mouth and stale cod fried so deep you could plaster a wall with it.

It's an exhausting city to walk unless you pause – mentally and physically – to take in lush flowers spilling from pots on cracked concrete balconies; cats prancing, purring and

23

napping on every block; aromas from across the Middle East and Europe clashing and clanging and somehow coming out perfect the way a hundred horrible voices singing in a medieval cathedral cascade into harmony.

Braided Tunisian "love ambassadors" strapped bracelets around our wrists crossing a lazy, busy square, and surrounded us to detach the bracelets when we chose not to give them money.

Though she was now a young adult, Maria smiled like a kid in a funhouse. She had decided over the years that I was decidedly uncool, the only question being whether I was the world's biggest dork or just a contender.

As anyone watching me write this would know, it more-than thrilled me to show Maria a place she found fascinating.

We ditched the midday sun for a tour of the Acropolis museum that our angel, Erato, arranged with her favorite tour guide.

Kay sat on a marble bench in the shade of a plane tree before entering the museum to give us her version of the ancient Trojan War. Plane trees have always been evocative to me: I picture the logician Aristotle in his white robes, the comic playwright Aristophanes holding court on a blazing day...

She put an arm around Maria whose black hair flowed to her shoulders: "Have you read Homer's *Iliad*? Good, then you know the story about how Helen, the most lovely woman in the world, ran off with Paris to the city of Troy and the Greeks spent 10 years trying to bring her back to her lovestruck husband. Don't believe a word of it, they're only trying to blame a woman for that stupid war. It's always our fault, isn't it? Men haven't changed their way of thinking in 10,000 years. Don't fall for it."

"What caused the war?"

"Tin and copper: Greece needed these metals to make bronze, Troy controlled the sea where they were shipped and kept raising taxes. Finally, the Greeks decided enough was enough. Think of your country's Revolutionary War: it was about liberty, not Britain's taxes, right?" Kay smiled and stepped into the sun. "The truth is never as romantic as the fiction. Men!"

Maria learned early not to believe every word a guy says, and for better or worse the guy was me.

She says it's the one thing she'll never forgive me for, and I suppose if there's only one, that's not so bad as a parent.

One day at breakfast I mumbled, "Ella malaka."

Malaka is a multipurpose Greek word that can mean anything from, "I miss you" to "dang, that bird flew away fast" to "go to hell."

Literally, though, "ella malaka" means "come here, you jerk off," with a more common translation to a disgusting term, as a long-ago Greek seaman explained to me on a grain freighter bound for Nigeria.

This would be a complex explanation for a five-year-old, so when Maria set her orange juice down and asked, "Daddy, what does malaka mean?", I told her, "Good morning; it means good morning."

In my defense, I'm certain thousands have used it exactly for the purpose of tossing a whimsical "good morning" to someone they love.

It happened to be Maria's first day of dance practice at the Greek Orthodox Church, where at a parking-lot festival the previous weekend she decided to become a Greek dancer.

Proud to show off her one Greek phrase to her new friends, Maria burst into the church with a brilliant smile and open arms:

"Ella, Malaka!"

Will she remember this? Even now, it might be only in my telling.

That afternoon at the Acropolis, I treasured the wonder in my kids' eyes. Many monuments are a letdown after the ubiquitous photographs and Rick Steves videos. The Acropolis is different because the photos never capture how breathtakingly it sits on a sheer cliff over the city.

A special treat for me was watching history roll across John's mind. While shoveling rock in Montana, the guy who found school too boring to even show up had listened to 16 hours of Yale professor Donald Kagan's podcasts about ancient Greece.

"Dad, getting money to build the Acropolis wasn't that different than trying to get the funds for a new football stadium in Minnesota," John told me, a sign of his budding interest in Finance. "They had to politic like mad to raise the money."

As the afternoon went on, I began to stumble like Socrates did on the way home from his legendary Symposia and his teaching gigs on top of this same cliff.

If you believe Plato, which I do, the Athenian old men drank nonstop while building the foundations for Western philosophy. They watered down the wine to keep their minds from going soggy too fast, and because it was well known that only barbarians drank their wine uncut.

Though I happened to be sober, I staggered like a drunk because I needed to arch my back to support my bobbling head.

The way I swayed back-and-forth down the street made a mockery of the Greek ideal of balance, at least in the battleground of my body. I addressed this by holding my chin up with my fist as I walked, stabilizing my posture and looking very much like the ancient philosophical master.

The hour is dusk in my romantic vision, with the sun setting crimson over the Acropolis and me striding (not fading!) into the sunset. In chronological truth, that silly construct, the sun over Athens was just striking 4 o'clock.

Still I hold the sunset in my memory, glowing softly on my face while my kids remain in the bright sunlight of optimism. My hopes are all for them, my love for them, my joy of watching them is what makes me want to live longer on this earth.

So for the moment let me walk like Socrates, on the streets he used to walk, let me pretend. Since just like Socrates, as dusk gathers I have more questions than answers, and that's the way he would have wanted it.

CHAPTER 6

The Perfect Storm

❧

The unexamined life is not worth living, the Greeks said. But sifting through memories and speculative theories that evaporate into the sizzling evening sky, the question is which part to examine.

Dogs bark and engines rev the way they do in every city. Across the street, people hustle in and out of Bobby's restaurant for souvlaki take-out until dawn. Tonight, instead of John and Nikos grabbing the food to go, the four of us head across the street for our late-night snack.

We change it up this time, ordering skewers of souvlaki chunks and tatziki dipping sauce rather than pita bread sandwiches, grabbing a table on Bobby's outdoor patio instead of taking it to go.

Bobby's regulars dine and guzzle Fix beer, laughing and stuffing roasted pork on skewers into their mouths as if feeding oneself is an easy and natural thing.

Nikos and John go to the cooler for cans of beer. Nikos isn't much of a beer fan, and John prefers crafts to generic ones, but here on Bobby's patio they can't imagine any beverage fitting the night more perfectly than a Fix beer. Neither can I, although Maria finds it easy to resist.

When I shift my beer can to my left hand because my right hand almost drops it, John's eye catches mine and we let the moment be.

From time to time, I ask the question my friends ask not only about ALS, but also about their own life-changing events: "How did this happen?"

My mom was the first to inquire about my deal in her sadness, and I'm not sure my attempt to soothe her did the trick: "Well Mom, unlike the rest of your kids, I didn't smoke enough dope."

Researchers at McGill University in Montréal believe there's something promising in cannabis. But to ease my mom's guilt, I suggested to her that marijuana deprivation might not have been the sole cause of my ALS.

I have alternately thought about the eel I ate from a river in Vietnam that was unfathomably polluted by American standards – toilet paper, newspaper, all sorts of paper and plastic and the occasional tree branch lurched their way downriver toward the sea.

The eel swam in circles and stared unblinking at us from the aluminum washbasin where it waited to be selected for lunch. Did it carry bacteria that made its way from my gut into my brain?

(When we left Vietnam, my sister-in-law asked me to delete the photo of the eel from my phone because it made her think of death. Did she know something that she didn't know?)

Sometimes late at night I think about three bloody bug bites I woke with on my right arm – the first to go – for five days straight in Mexico shortly before symptoms began. I almost had my room fumigated after the first night, but figured breathing that stuff could be bad for my health.

Later, my doctor Ann humored me by prescribing a drug used for Lyme disease with the caveat, "Just you know, I have zero expectation of this doing you any good."

"I agree," I said, "but I had zero expectation of getting ALS."

Do the roots go further back? Could it be soot from the L train that gathered as a fine metallic dust on my crib when I was an infant on the South Side of Chicago? Or the NSP powerplant on the Minnesota River in Burnsville where I grew up?

Maybe it was a genetic malfunction that hasn't yet been identified. Kicking off a month of unworldly coincidences,

Maria told me on the afternoon I let her and the boys know I had ALS, "Dad, I wrote a scholarship essay about ALS this morning."

"Well, that's spooky," I said. "Tell me what I have."

"My paper was about gene-editing for ALS. Scientists have found more than 20 genes that are linked to ALS," my 18-year-old daughter informed me. "It could theoretically be fixed in the womb. The fix would make no change to the embryo except turning off the ALS gene. But some ethicists seem to think preventing a disease before it starts is unethical."

Could the culprit be less controversial, like the hundreds of soccer balls I headed during practice in high school? Did a final straw break the neurons' back?

In the end, it's probably the perfect storm of many things combined with the predominant factor of age. The only sure thing is that time is running short. I suspect an effective treatment will come too late for me, but it will come.

This just in: I like my friend Teresa's theory best: "Everybody I've ever known who has ALS is incredibly smart. I asked my neurologist friend, and she said the same thing. The brain spins so fast the wheels fall off."

This is the most ridiculous of all theories, but ALS is a ridiculous disease so on a breezeless Athens night I'll take it :-)

The night is young for Bobby's takeout, just past midnight, and the patio is also filling up.

Somewhere between our first and second helping of souvlaki, Nikos asks, "If you knew this was coming, what would you have done different with your life?"

"Nothing that would have gotten in the way of meeting you guys."

CHAPTER 7

A Feast Fit for Odysseus

❧

When I first met Yannis, *Town and Country* magazine listed him as one of the world's three most eligible bachelors, although as a college sophomore I would question his eligibility for marriage.

He was, and is, brilliant, kind, self-effacing and just plain fun to be around, although he's also living proof that even the best of us aren't good at everything. One year over Christmas break, he called to ask if I lived anywhere near Iowa. I told him yes, it was one state over, so he booked a flight to spend a few days with my family in Minnesota.

For a week we played boot hockey under the moonlight at the ice rink behind the house where I grew up, and I believe this was the one thing I ever did better than Yannis. I attribute it to my natural talent rather than having grown up playing hockey. At the end of the week, he flew off to Idaho to join his family for a ski vacation... Idaho, Iowa, it's all the same to a global guy.

While I smoked him in hockey, Yannis clawed back on the academic talent front a few weeks later at Yale.

Late into the night before our Intellectual History course final, we holed up in a classroom where our roommate David – Summa Cum Laude and an accomplished leaper of parking meters, that lost art – gave Yannis an old-fashioned blackboard cram session while I hung out playing harmonica.

On our way to the exam the next day, a cold morning with rattling twigs and flecks of snow falling and blowing between Yale's neo-Gothic stone buildings, a tall gray-haired gentleman flipped his scarf back and gave David and me a grand hello.

"Who was that?" Yannis asked as snowflakes sprinkled courtyard trees.

"The professor," David informed the guy who had never quite made it to a 9 a.m. lecture.

Yannis scored highest in the 300-person class, with David second – leading to the eternal debate: Is Yannis that smart, is David that good a teacher, or was my harmonica playing proof that music is the greatest of all instructors?

Thirty-five years after college and my talents pretty much reduced to walking, talking and drinking wine, we gathered for dinner at Yannis' home outside Athens. This was shortly after the Paris nightclub bombing and the Turkish coup attempt. Yannis' wife Elena lovingly scolded him for flying home from Nigeria that night when the Paris airport was under high terror alert.

"Elena, I listened to you as always," Yannis assured her. "I didn't go through Paris. I went through Istanbul."

"Yannis, that's worse! The Turks blame America for the coup."

"Don't worry honey. I used my Greek passport," he answered. All Elena could do was shake her head – the Greeks and Turks have been at each other's throats for centuries.

During an open air dinner of roasted meats reminiscent of the feasts in the Odyssey that Athens night, Elena cajoled their kids and mine into discussing:

Trump or Clinton?

Bikini or Burka?

And a Greek twist on the question of local versus national lawmaking control: Can a Greek town decide whether or not to let a Greek and Turk marry, or is that a federal decision?

What's the best college major for somebody who wants to get into business? Accounting? Economics? A Business degree?

"History," said Yannis, the Intellectual History scholar. "History teaches us that every major event has somewhere between three and five primary causes. What is business about? Identifying what you want to happen, and what you need to do to make it happen."

The kids went to bed and Yannis and I opened what I believe was our third bottle of red wine from the Thessaloniki area in Greece's northeast.

With the clarity that comes under a moonlit sky and the exact right amount of wine, we got down to the business at hand.

"We've got to look at this logically," I said. "There's only one question that matters, as a parent: At what point am I taking more than I'm giving with my kids?"

"Never," Yannis shook his head.

"Not now, but the time will definitely come."

"They all need you around," Yannis insisted. "Maria is brilliant and beautiful and takes everything so seriously. She needs you to keep her light.

"Nikos lives in the clouds. He reminds me of somebody I knew at Yale – he's exactly like you, you know."

"He's actually a step or two better," I corrected my ex-roomie.

"Well, of course, but he needs you. He needs you to keep him grounded."

A woman poured more wine as they did in the ancient symposia, and Yannis continued, "And your son John, he's your rock. And he needs you more than you can even know. I see it in his eyes, in the way he watches you."

"You're still talking in the present," I told him. "I'm talking about the future."

Yannis shook his head again, "My father is 94 and breathing is all he can do now. He sits looking out over the Aegean Sea, and he breathes. Knowing my father breathes means everything to me. I tell you, everything."

I would think of that one later, when I had decisions to make.

Years ago when I was 20, I worked on one of Yannis' father's ships, a freighter carrying grain from Galveston, Texas, to Lagos, Nigeria, and returning to New Orleans.

I began as an apprentice officer doing mostly navigation. But this was the ocean, and there weren't a lot of hairpin turns, so I didn't focus well and worked my way down to being the engineer's assistant.

I hadn't realized how much of a ship is down below the water in the ocean. Unfortunately, I didn't like heights and much of the job had to do with walking along metal scaffolding over a hundred-foot drop.

So I exercised my downward mobility once again, becoming one of those guys who eternally scrapes the paint off the deck and repaints it. I romanticized this as my dream job, time to think under the infinite Atlantic sky.

The ships were built in Japan, and the decks were made of steel rather than wood. There was no tangible reason to paint and repaint the already heavily coated steel deck except to keep the sailors, a mixed crew of Greeks and Nigerians, busy so they wouldn't fight.

I thought I was solid at this job, but I found myself transferred to the role of cook's helper. This was clearly the best job on the ship.

The cook didn't want me messing in his kitchen, so I spent the day in the cooler minding my own business. This meant sipping Lowenbrau until it was time to drag a side of beef via a heavy chain to the kitchen and then get out of the cook's way.

Late at night when the other seamen were in bed, I moonlighted by leaning over the front of the ship and playing my Lowenbrau-fueled harmonica into the ocean waves. Flying fish danced to my melody.

I was excited to set foot on Nigerian soil, but first we spent a couple weeks anchored a mile offshore waiting for a spot in the port. I was put on overnight pirate watch, standing alone atop the deck, by the chief mate who hadn't particularly liked me from the start.

I received this honorable position, a lone seaman keeping the 400-foot ship, its crew and cargo safe from pirates, because I was the most expendable guy on the boat or, in my telling, the toughest.

What would I have done if pirates attacked? I must've had a plan and even instructions, but in my memory I had neither of these.

Much like the old man in Hemingway's novella who dreamt of lions sleeping on the white sandy beaches of Africa, my memory is suspect.

Memory is a ship anchored at sea, a mile off the coast, bobbing up and down and side to side, forever moving and forever still.

CHAPTER 8

Comfort in Numbers

This is all memory, and soon I will be too, and then I won't be anymore. Lying awake toward dawn, I run the numbers and they comfort me.

As with the Cycladic art museum we visited earlier that day with its 5500-year-old sculptures and figurines that look shockingly modern, analyzing my situation numerically puts perspective on how little my disease means in the context of history.

I don't mean my life has been worthless or meaningless or even unimportant. History teaches us every life is important, at least that's how I see it.

And numbers illustrate how little it means whether I die at 56 or 86.

An actuary told me that fewer than 10% of people in the history of humankind have lived past 55, putting me in the lucky zone. I question his math, considering the earth's population has exploded in recent years and he is probably straight lining the numbers over millennia, but I won't spend my limited time checking his work.

My comfort comes in this: at 55, the odds are I would only have about 15 years remaining where I would be mobile enough to travel the earth the way I like to do, walking cities until my shoes wear out.

If there's such a thing as life after death, those 15 years mean absolutely nothing as a percentage of eternity.

And if eternal life is a fantasy, if we're just molecules randomly banging around, those years mean even less.

A rooster crows in a vacant lot and I suppose I've been up thinking about this longer than I realized. Motorbikes rev, dogs bark, people and animals go about their lives. My mind smells coffee from the bakery down the block.

I shut my eyes to drift away for just a bit until my kids wake to start another day in paradise. By the time I get up and dressed, Maria is off for a solo walk through the neighborhood, locking into her memory pictures of kids climbing on and off school buses serenaded by grandmothers and dogs.

John and Nikos visit the bakery ladies one last time, returning with pastries and mystery coffees for breakfast on the sunny early morning balcony before leaving Athens.

CHAPTER 9

999 Steps above the Sea

"Erato, where do I leave the key?"

The angel spoke, "You can keep the key with you."

"We're leaving Athens today."

"Yes, I know, but we rented the apartment for the whole three weeks," she said. "We figured you and the children might want to leave your suitcases here in Athens so you can travel lighter to the mainland and the island."

"You're serious?"

"Of course."

This struck me as an obscene luxury and an unbelievably spot-on gift.

Nafplion, a southern seaport town on the Peloponnese, was our base for the next week of the trip. It was an easy drive from Nafplion to many of Greece's most compelling historical sites.

It was especially easy for me: John drove while I sat in the passenger seat, my right hand already too far gone for the stick shift. Life happens fast. In any case, John's five years navigating Montana's switchback mountain roads made him a better driver than me, good hand or not.

"Don't worry when I run STOP signs," he picked up quickly on rural Greek driving etiquette. "I'll slow down a little, but if I stop we'll get rear-ended."

Nafplion was just a short drive to Agamemnon's palatial compound at Mycenae, where ancient kings gathered and agreed to combine their armies for the Trojan War that was about... um, copper and tin.

And it's a day trip, taking the long way, to a village high in the mountains that hosted a surprise I would later jot down in a photo book as a miracle, if not a Miracle.

I had last been to Nafplion when I was 19 and now wanted to share its magic with my kids. I recalled a young curly haired Stathopoulos eager to breathe ancient air dashing up 999 steep steps along a winding precipice.

The Palamidi fortress stood at the top of the small mountain like a battered old giant, most interesting to my teenage self for the ways it was broken by time.

I remembered standing at the top of the cliff looking down over orange tile rooftops to the sea. Teal water in the horseshoe bay gave way to dark blue seawater, and I imagined waves of soldiers and migrants rowing long boats to these shores over thousands of years.

Now 36 years later, this rocky hike to the citadel was near the top of my list of things to do with my kids. They shared my passion for travel, for their Greek roots, and for the panoramic view we would get from the top. They also knew this was our last trip together.

We started midmorning to get the climb in before the sun got too hot. Nikos was tempted to sprint up the hill for the thrill of the run, but he hung with us for the greater joy of camaraderie and taking in the wildflowers and rocks and views along the way.

Twenty steps up, I paused to take in Nafplion from just a little above street level. Ten steps later I paused again, gazing at a rampart winding up a smaller hill across the street and a few hundred feet away.

I hadn't noticed that rampart my first time here, or maybe over three decades I wiped out the fine lines and kept the thicker ones. That was more likely.

Another 20 steps or so and I stopped to admire the flowers and aloe bushes that looked like fancy cacti to my Minnesota eye. Weeds captivated me everywhere, especially those adorned with bright little yellow or purple flowers that prospered in the desolate heat.

"How many steps?" I asked Nikos who, in addition to being a walking GPS, comes with a built-in counting machine.

"Seventy-two."

"Not even a hundred?" I squinted into the sun.

"More than 50," Nikos spoke the positive.

"You don't need to count for me," I told him. "Just enjoy the view."

"The counting happens in the back of my head. It doesn't distract me. I only pay attention when you ask."

Every time we rounded another curve up the hill, I stopped to gaze out at the city and the sea, gasping for breath.

Numbers weren't comforting me on our hike, unlike the ones that had given me peace the night before. Was I this out of shape?

"Don't wait, I'll meet you at the top," I told the kids, but they paused each time I stopped to breathe. Soon I started losing my balance on one leg, catching myself with the other. I thrust my left arm out the way I used to do with both arms to keep balance.

At first I found it funny, odd, whatever you want to call the sensation of a bird about to fly off a precipice. The higher we climbed, the more I swayed with each step. The path grew narrower, the drop steeper, and I noticed my kids looking back at me more often with concern in their eyes.

"How many?" I asked the lean human counting machine again.

"562," Nikos said.

"You guys go ahead," I beat back the part of me saying we were already more than halfway and I should keep on going. "I'll catch you at the bottom."

"I'll stay here with you," Maria walked down a few steps to where I slumped on a rock against the cliff wall.

"No, I've climbed it once. I want you to do it. You have no idea how much this means to me. I'll be in the café down the street."

We had passed a small café with outdoor picnic-style tables a block from the foot of the hill. I had a cold orange Fanta soda on my mind. Orange Fanta quickly became my daytime drink of choice in Greece, where by noon my body was a sandy thirsty beach.

My kids vanished around the next bend up the mountain. I sat with my back against the rocky wall propping my chin up with both hands admiring the rooftops, tall white sailboats and small fishing boats. A lone freighter took me back to when I had a working body, and an island out at sea evoked a time just three weeks earlier when I had dreams for the future.

Fifty steps from the bottom I found the ideal napping rock, a stone slab the length of a coffin and wide enough that I wouldn't roll off it if I fell asleep.

I clasped my hands behind my head and shut my eyes under tall thin-crowned pine trees. Sunlight dabbed my eyelids. A couple young kids came running up the steps, the mother scolding them in her British accent to slow down.

She stopped and asked me, "Are you okay?"

"Better than I've ever been. You have beautiful kids." They looked like they were about eight and 10 years old, excited to be climbing what I gathered was the biggest hill of their lives so far. "You'll want to keep them to the inside on the way up."

"Did you hear that?" She cautioned them and they ran laughing up the hill ahead of her. The sky above me through tall trees was dappled blue and white, and two crows circled high above.

My mind transformed the crows to falcons and I pondered how many Greeks, Venetians, Turks, Franks, Moors, you name it, called Nafplion home over the centuries and studied the universe lying on their backs right here.

They lived, they ate, they loved, they died.

Having climbed halfway up the hill only to come down for a nap and think momentarily about heading back up for another shot, I thought about the Greek half-god Sisyphus who pissed off Zeus with his arrogance – leading Sisyphus to mutter under his breath, "You're one to talk."

For this, Sisyphus was condemned to forever push a boulder up a mountain, only to have it roll down just before reaching the top. His torment was to wake up the next morning, every morning, and push the damn thing up again.

I wondered when the time would come that I would feel this way each morning, and what a relief it would be the day I let the boulder roll back down for keeps.

On that day, my soul would stand at the top looking out over the valley of life and, as they sing about the bear who went over the mountain, I'd see what I would see.

In the meantime, let me interpret the myth of Sisyphus differently. The story is not about futility. It's the opposite: Every time we push that boulder up the hill, we plant new seeds of life.

I picture eternally John, Nikos and Maria hiking to the top and to the Palamidi fortress, gazing out over the sea and imagining their future as I had at 19:

Nikos with his soul in the clouds while thoroughly enjoying his time on earth;

Maria with her feet on the ground and her mind shooting for the stars;

And John a bit of each, with a personality so welcoming that he never gets a chance to buy his own drink at a bar.

CHAPTER 10

Eternity

Wile my kids continued up the mountain that was a hill to them and everything to me, I stumbled in my newfound Socrates pose to the café down the street and took a bench at a sidewalk table. I thought about the coincidences that kept piling up on this vacation.

What an uncanny coincidence that the fertility fountain I desperately wanted to show my kids opened the season we arrived, after being closed for 20 years. I had no idea it had even closed.

Funny it was the day we visited the Acropolis that my neck weakened to the point I had to hold my chin up with my fist like a philosophical great.

Lucky coincidence that months earlier I booked flights for this vacation I had forever wanted to take with my kids, sensing there would never be a better time – only to learn five days before departure that it would be our last trip together.

How unlikely, and how eerie, that Maria had written an essay about ALS the morning I was diagnosed.

Yet to come, a wrong turn that led to something so right that it almost made me believe in, well...

At the sidewalk café near the foot of the 999-step hill to the Palamidi fortress, I propped my chin on my hands and rested my elbows on the table. I shifted on the bench so that I'd see my kids when they started down the street after descending the mountain.

I ordered a Loux brand Sour Cherry soda that tasted as unfortunate as our tour guide had warned me back at Delphi. Sour wasn't the solution to the dry heat. Still it was a pretty color even if it made me thirstier.

The guy who ran the café came out and I asked him in my awful Greek for an orange Fanta soda and a glass of Retsina, the Greek wine whose flavor I can best describe as the way melting tar on a street tastes to a child on a 100° day.

Suspecting correctly that I had pretty much blown my wad on the few words I knew, he asked me, "Are you French?"

"No, American."

"My name is Kostas."

"Peter," I raised my Fanta to greet him.

"Paniotes, you speak good Greek for an American. But unfortunately, you speak the wrong Greek. You should learn ancient Greek," he put his fingers to his lips and blew a kiss at the sky. "This is the language of the gods."

I recited the first line of Homer's *Odyssey* in ancient Greek and once again was at the end of my talents.

"You put most Greeks to shame and this is the problem," Kostas said. "Nobody speaks to the gods anymore. It's all about today, today, today... nobody cares about eternity."

"May I, please?" Kostas gestured to a bench across the picnic-style table from me.

"I would love it," I said.

A young man, maybe Kostas' grandson, brought out chunks of wood-grilled octopus and feta cheese drizzled with olive oil. He went back inside and returned with more food, a plate of warm pita bread accompanied by hummus, Kalamata olives and stuffed grape leaves.

He poured us each a glass of 80-proof ouzo, and dropped in an ice cube to unlock the flavor. "A chaser for your wine and soda," he nodded to my Retsina and Fanta.

I love stuffed grape leaves, or dolmades, and these were some of the best. They were chilled, filled with rice and herbs rather than the heated type that included meat, and came with a lemon sauce for dipping.

Kostas waved to a Greek Orthodox priest striding past our sidewalk table in his long black robe and a large silver cross on a necklace. The priest waved back.

"He's got to be hot as hell. Sorry, hot as heaven," I said. I sipped my ouzo where just a sliver of the ice cube remained in the dry heat.

"That man walks by at this time every day. I have no idea where he goes," Kostas nodded in the direction where the priest disappeared around a curve in the road.

"Are you Greek Orthodox?" I asked.

"I am a fish that swims in the Greek sea, so yes," Kostas said. "Are you?"

"I grew up Lutheran. My dad got kicked out of the Greek church."

He laughed, "What deadly sin did he commit?"

"He married a Lutheran."

"Ah, that's a bad one," Kostas nodded.

"You get the rest," I said. "Since they married in the Lutheran Church, according to the Greeks they weren't married at all. They were living in sin."

"And they produced you, Paniotes, a fine bastard child!" Kostas raised his ouzo glass. "To the Lutherans and to the Greeks."

"My favorite writer got kicked out of the church, too," I told Kostas. "I named my son Nikos after him."

"Kazantzakis, yes, a terrible heretic. He claimed Jesus gave up the possibility of a happy life with a wife and kids to save our souls. I can think of no sacrifice more moving."

I looked across the table into Kostas' eyes, bright blue as the marbles we used to play with as kids, and he went on: "People call the church God's house," he said. "But it's not. The church is our house honoring God. A place for us to come together and worship Him."

He sipped his ouzo and continued, "The people who run the church make mistakes. We all do. God doesn't. That doesn't stop me from going to church any more than a bad cut of meat every now and then keeps me from going to the butcher."

It was close to noon. The British woman and her two kids that I had seen in the morning now passed our table, returning from their hike to the fortress. She was sweaty and kept her eyes on the sidewalk in front of her, while her kids ran in circles.

The café began filling up with customers who, like us, had gotten a reasonably early start up to the fortress and were now ready for lunch. "Anything you'd like before I get back to work?" Kostas asked.

"Yes, I see my kids coming. It would be great if we could have three glasses of water waiting when they get here. Oh, and how about sending somebody out with a Coke, a Fanta and a lemonade."

"Our lemonade comes from a can," he said. "Our orange juice is fresh squeezed."

"Orange juice," I said. "Thank you."

"Anything else?"

"Yes, I'd love you to meet them when things settle down inside."

John, Nikos and Maria waved to me as they approached. If this moment could last, I thought, it would be close enough to eternity for me.

Customers kept pouring in, excellent for Kostas, so that was the last I saw him. His grandson, or whoever it was, brought out the beverages and we sat there in a slice of heaven.

CHAPTER 11

Just My Imagination

Woody Allen said Comedy is Tragedy + Time. A lot of other people probably said it, too.

How about the opposite? Tragedy is Comedy plus Time.

The hike partway up to the Palamidi fortress was an ending and a beginning for me. The ending was obvious, and the beginning was in the brightness on my kids' faces when they told me about going into an area of the fortress that looked like it hadn't been visited in some time.

"There was a chasm between the part where everybody went and the other part where we went – ruins that hadn't been repaired," Nikos described it to me. "But there weren't any Keep Out signs."

"We walked across a bridge made of two by fours. Dad, you wouldn't have liked it," John said. Later, he would tell me that when I was diagnosed with ALS, he immediately recalled my instability when we went mountain hiking in Montana two years earlier.

"How far was the drop?" I whisked a pesky bee away from our sidewalk table here in Nafplion.

"I don't know," Nikos shrugged, "500 feet?"

I was sure-footed once, had confidence in my body, confidence in my emotions and my mind. I still trust my mind. And I trust my emotions although I've grown to do so with a shaker of salt.

Lying on the rock slab earlier that day, however, I realized these, too, might be laid to waste like my body.

I remembered my grandma talking about little green men dancing in the grass outside her bedroom window. She knew they were imaginary and at the same time they were scary, real.

And what is real? The German playwright Goethe said he never wrote about anything he hadn't actually seen either with his eyes or his imagination.

I had some of each that night in Nafplion, the eyes and the imagination. Standing in my apartment bedroom after coming in from the balcony, a breeze through the screen rustled a pale red curtain that doubled as the closet door.

Something dark crouched in the closet, a silhouette behind the curtain. Did bony Death huddle in the corner, waiting for me to fall asleep? This was hilarious and I knew it. I also knew that someday I might not find it so funny: Twenty percent of people with ALS get a dish of dementia on the side. For now though, it was ridiculous.

Still, we all know what I did next. I pulled open the curtain to be sure.

It stood there in the corner of the closet, leaning against the wall.

A vacuum cleaner.

And a fisherman's cap above it, dangling from a hanger.

CHAPTER 12

The Turk

⚭

Every culture needs a foreign villain plotting to take it down. When I was a kid in Cincinnati, movies taught me who had America in their sights. But at five years old, I didn't have the historical context to know if I needed to keep an eye on the Russians, the Germans or the Martians.

Later, when I first started reading Greek history, I learned about the Persians who once had the largest army in the world. Twice in the 5th century BC, Persia tried to invade Greece. Among the many miscalculations the Persian kings made, the one that strikes me vividly is the color of their warriors' clothing.

Kings Darius and Xerxes should have clad their warriors in brown pants to disguise how quickly they filled them when running away from the Greeks who chased them out of the country.

The most notable villains for Greeks today, hands down, are the Turks. While I've personally never met a Turk I didn't like, there's a bloody history. The Ottomans occupied Greece until the 19th century, a 400-year horror that I could hardly imagine. More recently, in 1974 the Turkish army invaded the island of Cyprus which has been home to primarily Greeks since 1100 BC.

But it can get tricky telling one from the other. Ever since the two nations forcibly exchanged two million people in 1923, there have been more people with Greek family roots in Turkey, and more Turks in Greece, than either would care to admit.

In cultural solidarity with my people, I named my Turkish rug after my dear friend Gulsah so that I'd walk on a Turk each time I crossed my gathering room. Before leaving on this vacation, I promised to let her know if I spotted any of her type.

Our second night in Nafplion, it happened.

Nafplion's Syntagma Square is gorgeous. That's a simple statement, and it's just plain true. The public square in the middle of Nafplion's Old Town is surrounded by colorful neoclassical buildings and paved with gleaming marble.

The marble appeared pink to me when we first stepped onto it. Then it looked gray and I reminded myself that I tend to see the world through rose colored glasses when I travel. A few more steps and the marble was undeniably pink in the early evening light.

I soon discovered the square was paved in multiple colors. The marble's polish magically reflected streetlights and moonlight; lovers strolling arm-in-arm; teenagers kicking up their legs in an impromptu dance line; an old couple stuffing triangular cheese-filled tyropita pastries into their mouths; and their grandchildren unknowingly reenacting an 1822 battle with soft plastic swords that lit up until the batteries ran out.

We balanced two factors when deciding whether to eat dinner at a restaurant with outdoor tables located prominently in the square.

First, it was a great spot for people watching.

Second, the brick façade of the actual restaurant had words painted big and white in English above the door: Authentic Greek Food.

They say death and taxes are the two sure things in life. Equally certain is that if a restaurant announces in English that it has authentic local food, it doesn't. There might be exceptions, but I haven't found them. And any exception, if it did exist, would be filled with local diners.

We checked out the menu and it contained a decent array of Greek dishes: grilled lamb chops; lamb shoulder cooked with cinnamon; orzo pasta with shrimp; pork souvlaki; gyros and fries; fried calamari; grilled octopus; fried or grilled red mullet (more tastily called Barbounia in Greek); stuffed grape leaves; oregano baked chicken; a traditional Greek salad with lettuce, tomatoes, feta cheese, Kalamata olives and peppers; and an equally traditional tomato, cucumber and onion salad.

Despite never having experienced a great meal at a place shouting out its authenticity in any country, we opted for ambience and grabbed a table with a shimmering view.

The kicker for me was that the wine list included a dry red from Nemea. I had heard good things about Nemean wine. And the vineyards' proximity to Nafplion seduced a sucker for Greek myths and local beverages. Not many miles from where we dined, Hercules had performed one of his 12 Labors – slaying a Nemean lion.

"Is your Nemean red good?" I asked the host and got the inevitable answer.

"The best. It is the best wine in Peloponnesus. Maybe the best in Greece, who knows?"

Even if he said it was mediocre, I would've wanted to try it. We ordered a bottle of wine, appetizers and main dishes while the moon rose in the sky. The breeze was gentle, the laughter and music in the square were exhilarating, the appetizers were acceptable although the calamari was a touch mushy, and still after 30 minutes our wine didn't arrive.

"We're waiting for our wine," I reminded the host who doubled as our waiter.

"Yes, yes, I'm so sorry," he apologized. "I will bring it to you in five minutes."

He hustled into the restaurant, came out with our main dishes and served other customers, too. Another 20 minutes passed. "I think you might have spaced out our wine," I told him.

"Yes, yes sir. Right away," he rushed to the restaurant again and returned with the bottle. He poured glasses for each of us and hurried away to serve his other customers.

"This is terrible," I gave the kids my take on the flavor. "What do you think?"

"It tastes flat," Nikos said.

"It doesn't taste like it was ever good," I added while Nikos turned the bottle in his hands.

"Look at the label," he said. "It says fine WHITE from Nemea. They must have poured a different red into this bottle and thought we wouldn't know."

"They could've at least been smart enough to use a red wine bottle," John said and we all had a laugh.

After we returned home to Minnesota, I told Gulsah about our experience with her countryman.

"Why are you so sure it was a Turk?" Gulsah protested.

"Seriously, Gulsah, who else but a Turk would do something like that?"

CHAPTER 13

Women at the Beach

While the boys roamed the winding streets of Nafplion, Maria swam in pale blue waters off a rocky
outcrop from a beach after climbing a steel ladder down into the sea. Without arms strong enough to climb
or swim, I scanned the row of lounge chairs overlooking the
beach. All were taken.

The woman on the lounge to the left of me turned on her
side to check me out. She stared a moment and then gazed
past me at a pure blue sky with little white clouds.

Her smile widened for a moment before returning to its
closed-lip noncommittal pose. She shut her eyes, rubbed and
opened them again, and leaned over to take a yellow beach
bag, a pearly necklace and an aqua blue towel off the chair
beside her. She tapped her hand on the chair, "Please, sit."

"Thank you."

"Parakalos." (You're welcome.)

The way she wrapped the towel around her waist, and then removed and rolled it up to protect her eyes from the sun told me these were her things, and she had been waiting for somebody to come along that she could offer the chair. I'm not that handsome, so I must have appeared at least unobtrusive to have won this lottery.

I lay back in the chair and sat up when after a long time the waiter came around. I wanted to offer the woman who gave me her spare chair a drink, but her dark eyes hid under a towel and her lips held a closed contented smile I didn't dare interrupt.

The waiter took as long to deliver my drink as he had to come around in the first place, both of which I found refreshing. Eventually he arrived and I lounged back squinting at the sun sipping ouzo, the Greek liquor that old men sip all day, every day, under umbrellas at sidewalk cafes. The old men quench their hunger with chunks of octopus grilled over old wood, and shrimp that's netted and brought in straight from the harbor.

Ouzo is magical when sitting across the table from an old Greek man. Taken solo, it tastes like cheap licorice. Retsina wine, on the other hand, leads me to visit a young man. It takes my spirit back to when, as a young backpacker at a port town on the island of Crete, I drank my first wine ever – the horrid yellow Retsina that delivers less a hangover than a fever.

Way back then, I bought a glass for 20 cents worth of Greek drachma bills from a guy in a small wooden booth at the edge of a crowded park. It tasted odd but the wetness refreshed my tongue that hot dry afternoon, so I drank a couple more.

A bit sleepy after this, I laid down in the park's parched grass at dusk and woke alone under the stars at 3 a.m., the place now empty except for me and a few scraggly trees. I was 19 with eternity ahead of me.

I watched clouds float across the stars. Then I rose, stretched and walked back to Heraklion's port where fishermen motored in with the morning's first catches.

Nikos put it perfectly when he first sampled Retsina. He swirled it in his glass, watched its golden color absorb the sunlight, took a leisurely sip and said, "Dad, I like everything about this wine except the taste."

The beach in Nafplion where Maria swam with creatures we hadn't yet discovered, but that soon discovered her, caught the sunlight on her olive skin.

Rather than pristine grainy sand, the beach was covered in egg-shaped rocks bleached white by the sea and sun, with unstable wooden planks laid down to help people walk gingerly to the water.

The woman who had patted the chair and invited me to join her got up stretching her limbs theatrically and made her way toward the water. She looked back a couple times to see if I would follow.

But I was already at the point where my arms didn't fully work. Getting up from a horizontal position would have required more dorky lunges than I was up for in the heat.

Plus, it was so lovely just lying there watching her walk. She entirely and now unconsciously took joy in her body under the sun in the salty sea breeze.

She glanced down occasionally at her bare feet to make sure they remained on the wood planks that protected her from the jagged stones near the top of the beach. These rocks gave way to smoother stones worn round by the Aegean Sea though slippery and still not easy to walk on steadily.

She paused toward the end of the wood planks to look back at me over her shoulder one last time. She must've regretted giving up her precious second chair to someone who wouldn't even show his gratitude by joining her for a splash in the sea together.

I started to rise in my chair to get up, although that action didn't travel from my brain to my limbs. That day, the languid connection between my mind and body was slowed by the lazy sky and sparkling sea. In time the disconnect would grow more fundamental and nothing would bring it back.

The planks ended where the beach grew sandier right by the sea. She wiggled her foot to shake sand out of her flip-flop. Soon I won't even be able to do that.

The question reared its head again about what my life meant, and what it means, if anything, and for how long, O Grain of Sand that we all are.

The question gave way to a bright-lights memory of my old college roommate David leaping a parking meter on New York's 6th Avenue as we left the Radio City Rockettes' sky-high kicking show back when we were young dudes in Manhattan. David was a global investment banker who fantasized about running a corner general store in Canada, and I a guy who liked to play harmonica. I recall wondering which would be harder for me to master, the Rockettes' kicks or his parking meter leaps.

Now the woman from the lounge chair turns to look at me as she stands waist high in the sea. She lights a cigarette and I realize I did this all wrong – so careful, so healthy, so pointless when it came to ALS.

In 20 years she'll still be flicking those deadly ashes into the dirt and I'll be, well, the dirt.

Maria was quiet for the next couple days. She was a pensive young lady in the first place on that trip, observing more than she spoke although certainly not shy about talking. One thing

Maria did not like to do was give the time of day to pain or take pain killers.

This was the Greek way, a 70-year-old member of her dance troupe had told her, and Maria treasured the words of these women who were 30+ years ahead of her in their journey through this life. Socrates praised stories from old men at his symposia for the same reason: They were fellow travelers through time who gave him a glimpse of the road ahead.

Maria's aversion to letting anything so unworthy as pain get in the way of her day led me to take the expression on her face that morning extra seriously. I immediately stopped trying to figure out how many grounds to put in the coffee maker when she came to me in the kitchen of our apartment in Nafplion with a question in her eyes.

"Do you think I should have a doctor look at this?" she showed me a red spot near her shoulder, a bug bite with rings around it.

"Absolutely, let's go find one."

"I'm not sure it's a rush," she said.

"Anyway, I could use a walk," I told Maria so she wouldn't feel self-conscious. She hated putting anybody out, but I could think of nothing more precious than a morning stroll with her even if she didn't have a bug bite. We wandered away from the historic old town to a row of retail shops where we were sure to come across a pharmacy.

"Do you know where we can find a doctor's office?" I asked the pharmacist and Maria showed her the bite on her arm.

The pharmacist's English was marginally better than our Greek, and we roughly understood her description of where to find Dr. Kokkinos. After roaming 15 minutes with no luck except for time with a brilliant, curious and gorgeous girl, worthy in its own right, we realized how rough our understanding was.

Finally, after lapping the block checking names on street-front business doors that looked like they might house a doctor, we found Kokkinos' office on the ground floor of an old white wooden house.

The nurse-receptionist looked at Maria's arm, folded her hands on the counter and said, "You must tell me your name and then go sit down." I wondered if her bluntness reflected a dictatorial personality or the lack of subtlety that can come with speaking in a foreign language.

I said, "Stathopoulos" and started spelling S-T-A...

"It's okay," she waved a hand. "I understand. Sit down."

It was easy to peg us as Americans in Kokkinos' waiting room: We were the only ones not wearing T-shirts with what they considered to be American slogans.

While I wore a loose-fitting teal golf shirt and Maria a dark blue sundress, the people streaming in and out of the lobby and waiting area sported drab colored T-shirts saying,

"God bless America," "My other shirt is a beer," "are you my mother?" and more.

We weren't sure exactly what many of the people who came in through the front door were doing. Some dropped off paperwork, others picked up paperwork, some just lingered and then left, while others took chairs in the waiting room like us.

I noticed a handful of the guys who wandered in and out trying to catch Maria's eye. She neither engaged with them in a meaningful way, nor did she gaze sheepishly at the floor. Her response was polite and uninviting, a savvy that is important for a young woman who loves exploring foreign neighborhoods.

Two hours later, the receptionist/nurse stepped around the counter to tell Maria, "The doctor is ready. Come in."

Kokkinos was young and handsome under wavy black hair and a casual black T-shirt with no slogan. The nurse took Maria's blood pressure, pulse and temperature. The doctor pressed his finger on the skin around the red rings on Maria's arm.

"I am happy you came to see me," he said to her. "We will prescribe for you two medicines. One is to stop the hurting and the other is an antibiotic. Be sure to start the antibiotic right away. The spider that bit you is a cousin of the black widow. It is highly poisonous. Five percent of people die from this spider's bite."

As one who had already won the two in 100,000 ALS lottery myself, five percent was an astronomically big risk when it came to Maria. We hurried to a pharmacy where a woman in motorcycle gear took a break from stocking shelves, introduced herself as the pharmacist and filled the prescription.

A few days later at a beach on Hydra, a whitewashed island with 1200 donkeys and mules, 5000 cats and zero cars, I again sat in a lounge chair while Maria and this time my boys climbed down a ladder into the sea.

A blonde in a tight red bikini pressed her palms on the table where I sat with my drink. "You remember me?" she asked. I couldn't recall her from anywhere. "Try," she prompted me.

When that didn't illuminate things, she added, "We met in Nafplion."

This still didn't register so she added, "At Kokkinos." That's close to the Greek word for "red." Blame the baking sun, old age, or simply the fact that I've seldom taken much interest in remembering details: I futilely scanned the cafés and restaurants where we had hung out and came up with none that had anything like "red" in their name.

Maria climbed a ladder from the sea that lay behind this woman and ascended winding concrete stairs that I had attempted to descend a couple times. Both times, I turned back because my balance was already a few notches worse than it had been on our climb toward the Nafplion fortress just days ago.

As Maria rose from the sea behind her, this blonde Greek nurse whom I had sat 15 feet from in the doctor's waiting room on the mainland said, "I talked to Maria down by the water. I'm happy she's feeling better."

Forget the Oracle of Dead Tree. This living, breathing gateway to healing had followed us across the sea, from a white wooden house to a veranda table with a view.

Coincidence?

Of course it was, but that didn't stop me from doing what any good Ancient would do: Lean back with one more ouzo and scan Homer's wine-dark sea for little white fishing boats and quiet murmurs of hope that I might get to be part of Maria's life for many years.

What if this disease takes a wrong turn for itself and a right turn for me? It wouldn't be the first time a man cast a wish upon the Aegean and it came true.

On another sea not far away, Julius Caesar once said, "It's better to be lucky than to be good."

What if the old murderer got that one right?

CHAPTER 14

Two Wrongs Make a Right

For decades I believed my ancestors on my dad's side came from a Greek mountain village called Pyrgos on the Peloponnese not far from Olympia.

I based this on a letter my grandma wrote to my dad in the 1970s saying she didn't know why he would ever want to go to Greece. The people are poor and smelly and why did he think the family left?

Her letter rattled off a list of villages with the caveat that they might not even have the same names anymore – "you know what Greeks are like!" – and frankly might be abandoned because anybody with any sense would've gotten out and moved away.

She went on to note Greeks can't spell, and the letters of their alphabet made no sense in translation, but here are a few of the ways they might have spelled a particular town: Lagadia, Lagkadia, Lankadia for one; Rancuni or Racudi or maybe that was just another name for Lagadia or Lefkochori.

She suggested we also try Pyrgos or Pirgos, the village and not the city of Pyrgos. We would have been from the one without indoor toilets. There are eight villages with no toilets and that name in the Peloponnese alone, so good luck.

When I was 19 traveling from town to town, considering a good train to be an overnight one where I could catch some sleep rather than hitchhiking and yakking all night with a long-distance trucker, I sat with other travelers on a small stone patio waiting for a chronically late connecting train in the village of Pyrgos' station at the base of a mountain.

I had arrived at that particular Pyrgos only because it was where I switched trains after leaving Olympia en route to someplace else. A couple hours before dawn, our departing train pulled into the station. It was already packed, with no open seats. We piled bodies on bodies, warm and fully clothed, sharing a snapshot-happy coziness with people we'll never see again, which eventually applies to everyone we meet or maybe nobody. My destination was wherever I wake up.

The magic a mind can conjure! From that night on my relatives came from exactly that Pyrgos, and if it were daytime I would've been able to see their outhouse up the mountain. Who knows, maybe they had even put a toilet in the house since my grandma's long-ago letter.

Now 55 years old and using Nafplion, a former Venetian fortress town, as our base for visiting the Peloponnese region of Greece, I told the kids we would stop in Pyrgos the next morning to visit the ancestral hood on our drive to Olympia.

I still didn't know if this was technically the right Pyrgos, but that didn't matter. It was the feeling that counted. If any of our relatives were still there, they wouldn't know us anyway.

All the same, John and I sat on the couch late into the night, sipping bourbon and scrutinizing an old-fashioned paper map of the Peloponnese. We cross-referenced the map against the letter from my grandma to see if any of the other oddly spelled cities pointed geographically to a specific Pyrgos.

"What if it's not Pyrgos at all?" John said.

"Greece is a small country, but it's a pretty big haystack if we shift gears at this point," I smiled at the illogic of reversing decades of thought.

Still, we applied logic to our illogic. There are worse things to do on a warm breezy night with one's eldest son. And the past 40 years hadn't exactly been filled with thought about this topic; it was just a passive assumption.

The two L towns, whatever the correct spelling might be – and it turned out even the Greeks used several different spellings for them on the same road – were so close together on the map we decided to check them out.

I remembered hearing when I was 10 that my grandma and grandpa were from two villages very close to one another, rather than the same village. So it doubly made sense to investigate this possible two-for-one.

The last thing I did before going to bed was reroute the GPS on my phone to take the longer, inland mountain route to Olympia so that we would pass through Lagadia and Lefkochori on the way, in the morning.

We planned to arrive midmorning to ask around about anybody named Patsis or Stathopoulos – which I suspected was like asking if anybody knew a guy named Smith – before heading to Olympia to roam the site of the ancient games and sprint the track at dusk when it wasn't so blazing hot.

That would also get us off the unlit mountain backroads and onto the main highway before dark. I forwarded the route to John to queue up for the morning drive.

About two hours into our drive, the Ionian Sea sparkled on our left and the Taygetus mountain range rose higher in the distance to our right.

"We're going the wrong way," Nikos said, despite the Google Maps directions.

"I'll take Nikos over Google," John said. Many times over the years, Nikos had taken off like a walking map and we followed winding roads and trails to our destination. But this time we were too far into the route for it to make sense to turn back.

And only a fool would complain about a trip to the ruins of the original Olympic Games. Another perk to this drive was that it took us along the sea.

We arrived in Olympia an hour later without passing through any of the mountain villages my grandma mentioned: Lagadia, Rancuni, Lefkochori, Pyrgos or anything resembling those spellings except to the extent all Greek words sound the same to an American ear.

It turned out that when I forwarded the link to John's phone, Google Maps reverted to its default route, the most direct, skipping the L towns where we hoped our ancestors' bones and possibly their grandchildren lay.

Olympia was mystical, but unlike the ancient athletes basted in olive oil, it wasn't our main destination. It was worthy of a main event, though, for its broken beauty and its past when wars stopped momentarily across the known world for the Games.

Some things never change, even in the sporting world. In one of the first Olympic contests, a little-known runner named Orippus from the city of Megara won by tinkering with standard equipment in what we might call the original Deflategate.

He was accused of running naked to reduce wind resistance. In an "If you can't beat'em, join'em" world, Orippus' great victory inspired a thousand-year tradition of nude Greek athletes.

After exploring the site with our clothes on despite the heat, with our throats parched and soles moist, my kids lined up at the starting blocks for their Olympic sprint.

Each wore his or her chosen equipment: Maria sported a blue-and-white flowery sundress and red Keds sneakers. Nikos was clad in a purple T-shirt, khaki shorts and light blue Keds. And John went with blue jeans, a blue T-shirt and dark hiking shoes. He set his sunglasses on a rock so they wouldn't fly off with his speed.

John and Maria gunned it to the end of the field and walked back casually jubilant with their arms in the air.

Nikos sprinted to the end and back, not stopping but just swiveling when it was time to turn around, barely breaking a sweat, in my mind putting even the ancient Orippus to shame because he achieved this fully clothed.

Their old man hoisted his butt up onto a boulder and watched, hand on his chin, teary hearted even if not teary-eyed.

Leaving Olympia with dry mouths and dusty legs in the late afternoon, we grabbed several bottles of strawberry and grape Fanta, Sprite and Coke at a small grocery store. We left town with the car windows down, hitting the highway fast to quickly circulate fresh air until the air-conditioning kicked in.

"Should we give those mountain towns a try?" I asked.

"Let's do it for the view if nothing else," John said, a man of my own heart.

He sped two hours up twisty narrow mountain roads and switchbacks, maneuvering like a crazy Greek to avoid being hit by crazy Greek drivers.

As the sun began to set orange over the mountaintops we approached Lefkochori, the last town on the route to Olympia we had plotted out on our paper map the previous night. Because the GPS took us the opposite direction, it was now our first stop on the way from Olympia back to Nafplion.

A shed made of sheet metal leaned into a cliff to our left. An old white tractor and a faded blue pickup truck with the sort of small bed you see buzzing around southern Europe rested in the brown grass and looked like they'd been resting a long time.

The cliff rose to a steep mountainside dotted with other sheds. Or maybe those were small houses where our relatives lived. It wasn't clear.

With night approaching and no obvious path up the mountain from our road, we decided to head on, the kids' legs still dusty from their Olympian sprint. John navigated the narrow winding highway with cliffs hugging the left shoulder and a drop of thousands of feet to our right.

He deftly dodged a fruit truck careening down the curvy mountain road, pulling so close to the edge without slowing that I caught myself leaning to the left in our passenger seat for body weight.

"We come from goats," I explained and understood what my grandma meant about leaving.

I hated heights, although they saved our ancestors: Thanks to its tough landscape and its distance from large cities that would be trophies in a war, few invaders reached this section of the Peloponnese.

In that sense the jagged mountains served my kids and me well, too. If the Ottomans, Venetians, you name it, had over-run these villages, we wouldn't exist or would at best look funny like they do.

We looked down from Lefkochori over a small village in the valley far below, accessible by different roads that ran comfort-ingly flat along the river. But the low land wasn't our route. We continued along the high road that leaned gradually down toward Lagadia, our second stop, three miles away.

We reached Lagadia around dusk, entering from the oppo-site side we had planned when looking at the map the previ-ous night. We arrived at an entirely different time of day, too, almost dark and with shops soon closing.

John's eyes were dried out from our Olympic adventure followed by his mountain drive into the sun. Finding traces of anything here was a long shot, and we were all drenched by the heat, so we decided to keep our visit to Lagadia brief:

Stretch our legs, stretch our eyes by letting them gaze over a deep valley to the next set of mountains, and then head back to our apartment after a memorable day.

The village of 355 people, down from 3,333 back in 1949, brought nostalgia even to one who had never been there: a couple of cafés, a couple of churches, a couple cemeteries, a one-room general store, and a sign that said "POLICE" over an archway but no indication a cop had been around in years.

The mountainside ascending from the main street held a few dozen houses, although the drop to our right was too steep. We parked at an overlook after passing through the town. The sky over the mountains across the valley turned purple-gray.

Maria walked away, her Olympian sundress swaying with joy, to check out a marble obelisk with names chiseled in black of locals who died defending Greece in "THE WAR."

No Stathopoulos and no Patsis, except one name looked a little bit like Patsis could if the original transcription to our alphabet had been horribly sloppy. Even then, it would have been a stretch.

But as we all knew from my grandma's faultless letters, Greeks can't spell.

Maria traced her finger along the engraved letters of that name.

Lagadia was book-ended by cemeteries. We set out on foot to the one we had passed while driving into the village because a stroll sounded nice and it was the first one we'd seen.

Posing for photos with wildflowers and donkeys, we made our way leisurely across this one-block, 12 donkey town to the small cemetery at the edge of a cliff behind a pretty chapel.

While John, Maria and I systematically paced crooked rows reading gravestones, the human GPS strode immediately to a raised tombstone marked "Antonios Stathopoulos."

The stone held a faded Polaroid of Antonios along with his dates of birth and death. This man appeared to be a few years older than my grandpa Paniotis Stathopoulos and died a decade after my grandpa.

We all stared at the gravestone, then at each other, and back again to the inscribed stone.

"My grandpa had a brother who taught Math at the University of Athens," I shared the only possibly relevant information I knew. Athens was a five-hour drive from Lagadia and might have taken days back then through tenuous mountain roads.

"What was his name?"

I shrugged. Antonios rang true, although in that moment any name we found in this magical setting would ring a bell.

"Does it matter if it was him?" Maria echoed my sentiment but with a hint it wasn't just rhetorical to her.

"It's the feeling that counts, and I have it," I had been arbitrarily content with Pyrgos for 35 years, so why not Lagadia?

"We can look online," Maria said. "We might not find anything because it was so many years ago. But if we do, that would be cool."

"What if we find out it wasn't him?" I asked.

"Nothing can prove for sure it wasn't him," Maria assured me. "But if we prove it is..."

John got bored with the discussion and wandered away, as he tends to do with detail, a genetic oops he got from me.

He stood a block away diddling with canes and walking sticks in a barrel outside the town's general store. When we eventually meandered that way too after breathing in the sacred air of possibility, soft-spoken John was waving his phone and gesturing with his hands to a guy about my age behind the counter.

"Familia?" we heard John say, aiming for a word they might both understand and sliding his phone across the counter.

The man's olive face went pale and he called to an older guy, a white-haired customer across the store. They flailed their arms around while raising their voices the way Greeks do, grabbing the phone from John and studying it closely.

"How do you know this man?" the guy with white hair tapped the photo of the gravestone on John's phone.

"Familia," John said rather than asked this time.

"Your familia?" the customer asked John and translated my son's "Yes, my familia," for the shopkeeper.

He explained the wonder on the shopkeeper's face, "The man on your phone: He was this shopkeeper's Mathematics professor at the University of Athens in 1971."

"Your professor 45 years ago was my grandpa's brother," I closed the loop.

"Little Paniotis was your grandfather!?" White Hair exclaimed. "His brother Antonios talked about him all the time. He moved to Milwaukee, America, no?"

Maria's eyes widened and she looked at me.

"We are all familia!" the customer twirled his finger in a circle above his head and the shopkeeper followed suit.

A sort of dance broke out and I snapped a photo of them aping in the general store: my three kids, Antonios' math student and the old man with white hair.

It's the most precious photo I have, and I like the fake even better: That night I emailed the photo to a friend asking if he could work me into it.

Thirty minutes later he shot it back, replacing the face of the smiling white-haired gentleman with mine. So now it was my kids, the student of my grandpa's brother, and me.

Does it matter that I wasn't the guy in the original photo?

No.

Does it matter this was the actual village my grandpa walked and left when he was my twins' age?

Yes.

Don't ask me why.

This chance meeting happened only because we tossed aside decades of certainty to change direction at the last moment, traveled the wrong route and arrived at the wrong time of day on the wrong side of town.

I whispered in the town square by the obelisk, "Almost enough to make a guy believe in miracles."

Almost.

CHAPTER 15

Life's Meaning in a Smile

We're enjoying our last few days in Greece in a rustic villa on the island of Hydra. The haphazard villa overlooks orange tile rooftops, brilliant white houses and a horseshoe-shaped harbor packed with sailboats, rowboats and fishing boats.

No cars are allowed on Hydra, the perfect place to wind down our trip after noisy Athens and our driving tour around the Peloponnese.

The Greek economy is famously in shambles. I'm haggling with a shopkeeper along the harbor about the price of two beer mugs I'm picking up for a couple guys I work with back home.

"These are nine euros apiece," she says, "so that's 17 euros."

"Eighteen," I correct her unnecessarily generous math.

"You're buying two," she puts on her game face and drops the price again. "That means a discount, 16 euros for you."

She wraps the mugs in newspaper and tucks them into a snug bag so they won't break. I hand her 20 euros and hustle out of the store. She chases after me with a five euro bill: "Your price is 15 euros for two."

The shopkeeper had tried to lower her price even after making the sale. One could read this in a lot of ways, including shaking your head and saying no wonder their economy is trash. I read it with a smile and a desire to believe in karma the same way I'd like to believe in miracles.

Alone at midnight sitting on our Hydra balcony, I take in the harbor covered in blackness with silver lights sparkling the sky. The villa where we're staying is fairytale disjointed:

To go from the bedrooms where Nikos and Maria sleep to the kitchen and dining room, you walk outside on a walled stone path surrounded by aromatic flowering vines. The blue-and-white tiled bathroom and shower are along the walled path, too. So are the washer and dryer, and the washing machine hose drains onto the bathroom floor.

John hasn't come home yet. He stayed at the Veranda restaurant up the mountain playing chess with the bartender into the night after we left. They played for bourbon, although he poured for John win or lose.

Toward 4 a.m. John jumped off a cliff into the sea with a Dutch couple who also closed the place down. It's a night he'll never forget, one he'll someday tell his children about.

My kids have enjoyed every day of this trip. I've seen it in their smiles, and in their step, and heard it in their voices. This means more to me than anything, and I mean anything.

The question of any meaning beyond this dissipates into a word game, nothing more.

The night is soft and the patio where I sit alone smells of midsummer flowers and faintly of the sea. I take a deep breath to register simultaneously that I'm alive and dying, something I should have done more often all my life.

Oddly, I have no major regrets; just a few small ones: The kind word I didn't get around to saying, the times I didn't make time to play trucks.

My phone lights and I have a message from a woman I met when we were both seven, was obsessed with in my early 20s and who remained a friend throughout the years as our lives went different directions.

Her message is simple: "I'm going to write the most beautiful love story. Will you write it with me?"

ACKNOWLEDGMENTS

Special thanks to...

Erato for taking logistics off the table so we could simply enjoy our vacation.

Merit Cudkowicz, MD, Chief Neurologist at Massachusetts General Hospital and Harvard Medical School, for sharing her knowledge and hope with me personally, and for leading research initiatives that could change the game for everyone with ALS.

Jeff Kleinman, Founding Partner, Folio Literary Management; Brian Defiore, President, Defiore & Company literary agency; and family and friends Eric Gutierrez, Joe Reger, Elaine Stathopoulos and Cathy Yandell, for their insights into these stories as part of a broader piece.

Rosemarie Reger-Rumsey, David Klass and Dr. Perri Klass for introductions that led to stories in this collection appearing in the St. Paul Pioneer Press (Mike Burbach) and New York Times (Roberta Zeff).

Mike Pickett for building my upcoming blog.

Jennifer Hjelle and Marianne Keuhn at the ALS Association MN/ND/SD Chapter for checking select facts and all they do toward knocking ALS out.

The Burnsville High class of '79 dogs and my Yale '84 roommates for endless warmth and laughter.

Bobbi Oates, Anastasia Demehin, Sara Rebhorn and Amy Casura for the much-treasured vacation photo book.

Betsy, John, Bev and Jim Stathopoulos, Mabrouk Yahya and Fadumo Jama for going beyond the call of duty every day.

Dave Wicker for showing us all how to live and give during life's extra innings.

CPSIA information can be obtained
at www.ICGtesting.com
Printed in the USA
LVHW011733271020
669965LV00014B/2194